I am Helen Keller

ORDINARY PEOPLE CHANGE *the* WORLD

BRAD MELTZER
illustrated by Christopher Eliopoulos

DIAL BOOKS FOR YOUNG READERS • an imprint of Penguin Group (USA) LLC

I am **Helen Keller.**

When I was little, I was just like you.
I loved to play.
I loved my dog.
And I loved seeing all the bright, beautiful flowers.
I also loved copying people. At six months old, I could
already say...

On the day I turned one, I started walking.
Oh, and there was another word I always loved.

Just like any other kid, right?
But there's one thing that made me different.
When I was nineteen months old, I got very sick.
The doctors said I wouldn't live.
I did live, but the sickness made me blind and deaf.

This is how I see the world.

Close your eyes and block your ears.
I couldn't see anything.
Or hear anything.

That's right.
Nothing.

I know it seems scary.

It was scary for me too.

Back then, people didn't know how to deal with someone who was deaf and blind.

My relatives thought I was a monster.

They were right: I wasn't well-behaved. I was extremely frustrated. In my dark world, I couldn't tell if anyone noticed me or cared about me.

I couldn't see or hear what I was doing.

But by the time I was five, I'd figured out small ways to communicate.
To say YES, I nodded my head.
For NO, I shook it from side to side.

To say FATHER, I motioned
to put on his glasses.

For MOTHER, I rested my
hand on my face.

For my baby sister,
I did this...

And when I'd shiver like I
was cold, it really meant...

But even with those signs, I couldn't get my dog, Belle, to play with me.

I didn't know how to speak, so I couldn't call her.

I just wanted to play with my dog.

The saddest part was, I got used to a dark and silent world.

People told my parents to give up on me. That I'd never be good at anything.

They didn't listen, though.

After reading about another blind and deaf girl, my parents found something they hadn't had since I'd gotten sick.

Hope.

We *all* do.
Everyone needs a teacher.
Still, I had no idea what the world was about to bring me.

I never had a more important day.
I was six years old.
From the way my mother was hurrying, I knew something
big was coming.
I stood on the porch, waiting, feeling the sun on my face.

Someone approached—I could feel footsteps.
I reached out, thinking it was my mother.
She pulled me into her arms.

Her name was Anne Sullivan.
She's the teacher who
changed my life.

In one of her first lessons, she gave me a toy doll. After letting me play with it, she spelled the word DOLL into the palm of my hand.

I could feel them.
But I didn't know what letters or words were. Or how they worked.

It didn't stop Miss Sullivan.

One day, we were arguing as she was trying to teach me the words MUG and WATER.

I got so upset, I took my new doll and smashed it on the ground.

I got angry a lot back then.

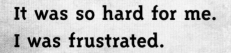

It was so hard for me.

I was frustrated.

Never losing her patience, my teacher took me outside.

At a nearby spout, she put my hand under the running water.

In my other hand, she spelled the word. W-A-T-E-R.

Then she spelled it again.

W-A-T-E-R.

W-A-T-E-R.

W-A-T-E-R.

From there, I realized that everything had a name.
Every object I touched seemed to burst to life.

And now, when I wrote words in my teacher's hand,
I had someone who could understand me.

When you're learning something new, it's often hard.
I started with words.
My vocabulary grew fast.
Eventually, I learned the meaning of the word LOVE.
I had given my teacher some flowers. So she spelled into my hand...

"It is here," she spelled
while tapping at my heart.
I was still confused.
It was hard to
understand something
I couldn't touch.

It made no sense.
Why couldn't my teacher show me love?
But then, she explained...

There, in that moment, my whole world changed.
It was as if there were invisible lines that stretched between me and everyone else in my life.
Close your eyes.
You can feel it too—your connection to your family and friends.

Still, life was never easy.

Without sight, I couldn't see people's faces.

Without sound, I couldn't hear their voices.

But one of my greatest breakthroughs came when I learned to do what you're doing right now.

Reading.

To practice, I'd match each word with its object and make sentences.
This was my favorite game.
We played it for hours.
See if you can find the sentence: Girl is in wardrobe.

From there, I started reading real books.

Just like you.

The only difference was, my books were in Braille, which is a series of raised dots that you read with your fingers.

Go ahead and try.
Move your pointer finger over the dots below.

At first, it just feels bumpy, right? You'll get used to it.
These dots spell my name. H-E-L-E-N.

Want to read *your* name in Braille? Here's the alphabet.

Run your pointer finger over the letters. Now close your eyes.

There you go!
Now you're reading just like me.

A	B	C	D	E	F
G	H	I	J	K	L
M	N	O	P	Q	R
S	T	U	V	W	X
Y	Z				

To make reading even more fun, my teacher took me outside. She knew I loved feeling the sun on my face and smelling the pine needles.

I read my books so many times, I wore down the raised dots.

There were *The Arabian Nights*, *Robinson Crusoe*, and one of my favorites, *Little Women*.

In those pages, I met brave boys and girls who could hear and see.

"I AM NOT AFRAID OF STORMS, FOR I AM LEARNING HOW TO SAIL MY SHIP."

One of Miss Sullivan's best lessons came when she showed me how plants grow.

FEEL THESE BUDS.

SOME BUDS OPEN FAST.

OTHERS OPEN SLOWLY.

A FLOWER CAN ONLY BLOOM IF IT'S WATERED.

When I was nine years old, I wanted to learn how to speak.

Even Miss Sullivan was worried about teaching me. She thought I'd get frustrated. But nothing would stop me now.

To help me, Miss Sullivan took me to a teacher named Sarah Fuller, who would put my hand to her face and let me feel her tongue and lips as she made each sound.

YES, HELEN.

FEEL EACH SOUND. LIKE THE VIBRATING STRINGS ON A PIANO.

In an hour, I learned the letters M, P, A, S, T and I.

MA.

Now I could call my dog, and she'd come to me.
At my seventh lesson, I spoke this sentence,
the one sentence that I'd repeat over and over:

As I got older, I didn't just learn to speak English.
I learned French and German.
For college, I wanted to go to Radcliffe, at Harvard University.

At Harvard, most of my books weren't available in Braille,
so Miss Sullivan spelled out many of the textbooks in my hand.
That's how much I loved learning.
And that's how patient and selfless Miss Sullivan was.

I became the first deaf and blind person to earn a college degree. I wouldn't be the last.

As I grew older, I wrote twelve books and visited thirty-four countries.

But the most important thing I did was to make sure that other people with disabilities could get the same education I had.

That was only the beginning.
I didn't just help the deaf and blind.
I started fighting for social change: to help women vote, to help the poor survive, and to help people who needed it most.

SHE WAS ONE OF THE EARLIEST SUPPORTERS OF THE ACLU, TO FIGHT FOR FREE SPEECH.

SHE WAS ALSO ONE OF THE FIRST SUPPORTERS OF THE NAACP, TO HELP BLACK PEOPLE GET EQUAL RIGHTS AS WELL.

SHE MET EVERY PRESIDENT FROM GROVER CLEVELAND TO LYNDON JOHNSON.

BUT LET'S BE HONEST.

THEY MET *HER*.

Today, the American Foundation for the Blind and Helen Keller International continue to help the blind and hungry.

In my life, they said I was different.
They said I'd never be normal.
But the truth is, there's no such thing as a "normal" life.
Every one of us is like a flower that must be watered.
Every one of us is full of potential.
And every one of us can overcome obstacles.

Look at me.
Hear my words.
I may not be able to see, but I have vision.
I may not be able to hear, but I have a voice.

Think of your life as a hill that must be climbed.
There's no correct path to get to the top.
We all zigzag in our own ways.

At some point, you'll slip,
  you'll fall,
    you'll tumble back down again.
But if you get back up and keep climbing, I promise you...

You will reach the top.

Don't let anything hold you back.
Our lives are what we make of them.
There will always be obstacles.
But there will always be ways around them.

I am Helen Keller
and I won't let anything stop me.

"*The best and most beautiful things in the world cannot be seen or even touched, but just felt in the heart.*"
—**Helen Keller**

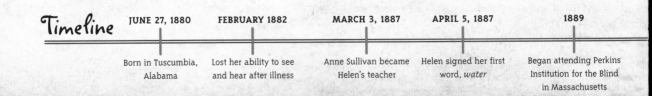

Timeline

JUNE 27, 1880	FEBRUARY 1882	MARCH 3, 1887	APRIL 5, 1887	1889
Born in Tuscumbia, Alabama	Lost her ability to see and hear after illness	Anne Sullivan became Helen's teacher	Helen signed her first word, *water*	Began attending Perkins Institution for the Blind in Massachusetts

Helen, age 8,
with Anne Sullivan

Helen with her
Boston terrier

Helen "hearing" Eleanor
Roosevelt by touching
her moving lips

1890	1903	1904	1924	OCTOBER 20, 1936	SEPTEMBER 1964	JUNE 1, 1968
Sarah Fuller began teaching Helen to speak	Published her first book, the autobiography *The Story of My Life*	Graduated from Radcliffe, the women's college at Harvard	Began work with the American Foundation for the Blind	Anne Sullivan died	Was awarded the Presidential Medal of Freedom	Died in Easton, Connecticut

For my ninth-grade English teacher,
Sheila Spicer,
the very first person who told me I could write.
Thank you for believing in me,
and for proving the true power
of a dedicated teacher.

—B.M.

For my lifelong friend, Dr. Vincent Pizzuto.
Vinnie, since the day we met when we were 5
until this day, you have made me want to be a
better person. Not by what you said or did, but
by being the person you are. You taught
by example and I love you for it.

—C.E.

Special thanks to Helen Selsdon at the American Foundation for the Blind
for all her help in getting the details right.

SOURCES
The Story of My Life by Helen Keller (Signet, 2010)
My Story by Helen Keller (CreateSpace Publishing, 2014)
Helen Keller: A Life by Dorothy Herrmann (Knopf, 1998)
Lies My Teacher Told Me: Everything Your American History Textbook Got Wrong
by James W. Loewen (New Press, 2008)
Helen Keller: Activist by Rachel A. Koestler-Grack (Chelsea House, 2009)
Helen Keller International (www.hki.org)
Helen Keller YouTube Channel (www.youtube.com/watch?v=8ch_H8pt9M8)

FURTHER READING FOR KIDS
Helen's Big World: The Life of Helen Keller by Doreen Rappaport (Hyperion, 2012)
Helen Keller: Courage in the Dark by Johanna Hurwitz (Random House, 1997)
Who Was Helen Keller? by Gare Thompson (Grosset & Dunlap, 2003)

DIAL BOOKS FOR YOUNG READERS
Published by the Penguin Group • Penguin Group (USA) LLC, 375 Hudson Street, New York, New York 10014

USA | Canada | UK | Ireland | Australia | New Zealand | India | South Africa | China
penguin.com

A PENGUIN RANDOM HOUSE COMPANY

Text copyright © 2015 by Forty-four Steps, Inc. • Illustrations copyright © 2015 by Christopher Eliopoulos

Library of Congress Cataloging-in-Publication Data
Meltzer, Brad. • I am Helen Keller / by Brad Meltzer ; illustrated by Christopher Eliopoulos. • pages cm. — (Ordinary people change the world) • ISBN 978-0-525-42851-0 (hardback)
1. Keller, Helen, 1880–1968. 2. Deafblind women—United States—Biography—Juvenile literature. 3. Deafblind people—United States—Biography—Juvenile literature.
I. Eliopoulos, Chris, date, illustrator. II. Title. HV1624.K4M45 2015   362.4'1092—dc23   [B]   2015000613

Photo on page 38 courtesy of Whitman Studio/Library of Congress. Page 39: photo of Helen with Anne Sullivan courtesy of the New England Historic Genealogical Society, www.americanancestors.org;
photo of Helen with dog courtesy of the Library of Congress; photo of Helen with Eleanor Roosevelt © Corbis.

Manufactured in China on acid-free paper • 10 9 8 7 6 5 4 3 2 1
Designed by Jason Henry • Text set in Triplex • The artwork for this book was created digitally.
The publisher does not have any control over and does not assume any responsibility for author or third-party websites or their content.